DOMINOES

Perseus

QUICK STARTER 250 HEADWORDS

OXFORD
UNIVERSITY PRESS

Great Clarendon Street, Oxford, OX2 6DP, United Kingdom

Oxford University Press is a department of the University of Oxford.
It furthers the University's objective of excellence in research, scholarship,
and education by publishing worldwide. Oxford is a registered trade
mark of Oxford University Press in the UK and in certain other countries

First published in Dominoes 2012

2025 2024 2023 2022

15

No unauthorized photocopying

ISBN: 978 0 19 424937 9   Book
ISBN: 978 0 19 463904 0   Book and Audio Pack

Audio not available separately

Printed in China

This book is printed on paper from certified and well-managed sources

ACKNOWLEDGEMENTS

Text adaptation by: Bill Bowler

Cover artwork and illustrations by: Janos Jantner/Beehive Illustration Agency

The publisher would like to thank the following for permission to reproduce photographs: Shutterstock
pp. 24 (Clash of the Titans, 2010 Sam Worthington Louis Leterrier (DIR)/Jay Maidment/
Warner Bros/Kobal), 25 (Beowulf, 2006 Ray Winstone Robert Zemeckis (DIR)/Moviestore).

DOMINOES

Series Editors: Bill Bowler and Sue Parminter

Perseus

Retold by Bill Bowler

Illustrated by Janos Jantner

Bill Bowler studied English Literature at Cambridge Universtiy and mime in Paris before becoming an English language teacher, trainer, and materials writer. He loves the theatre, opera, ballet, cinema, history, art, storytelling – and travelling. He also enjoys reading books and writing poetry in his free time. Bill lives in Alicante with his wife, Sue Parminter, and their three children. This Dominoes retelling of the Perseus story is based on Greek and Latin versions of the tale.

OXFORD
UNIVERSITY PRESS

Story Characters

Perseus

Perseus's grandfather,
King Acrisius

Perseus's mother,
Danae

Perseus's father, Zeus,
king of the gods

Dictys,
a fisherman

King Polydectes

Medusa and
her sisters

The goddess
Athena

The god
Hermes

Princess
Andromeda

The Grey Sisters

The Nymphs of the
Fountain

The sea monster
Cetus

Contents

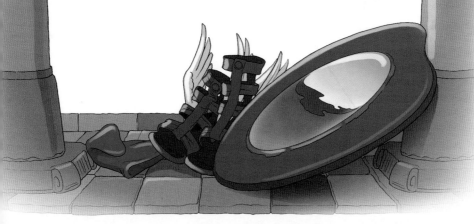

BEFORE READING

1 **Perseus is a young man from Greece. His story is very old. What do you think happens in it? Tick the boxes.**

a Perseus must find a present for....
   1 ☐ his mother
   2 ☐ a fisherman
   3 ☐ King Polydectes

b Perseus has help from....
   1 ☐ a sea monster
   2 ☐ the god Hermes
   3 ☐ the sea god Poseidon

c Perseus visits....
   1 ☐ the home of the gods
   2 ☐ three islands
   3 ☐ the country of the dead

d Perseus marries....
   1 ☐ the goddess Athena
   2 ☐ Medusa
   3 ☐ Princess Andromeda

e Perseus kills....
   1 ☐ his father
   2 ☐ his mother
   3 ☐ his grandfather

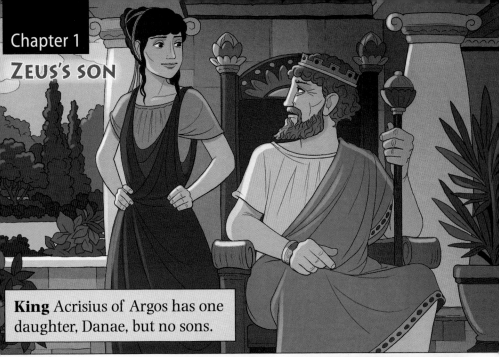

Chapter 1
ZEUS'S SON

King Acrisius of Argos has one daughter, Danae, but no sons.

He goes and asks the **priestess** at Delphi, 'Can I have a son?'
She answers, 'In my **fire** I see your grandson years from now. He kills you, and is king after you. Don't ask for a son, my king.'

Back in Argos, Acrisius thinks, 'But Danae, my daughter, can **marry** and have a boy!'

king the most important man in a country

priestess a woman who can talk to the gods

fire this is red and hot, and it burns

marry to make someone your husband or wife

So he puts Danae in a **tower**. Nobody visits her. How does she feel? Very bad. From the sky, Zeus, the king of the **gods**, watches. He likes Danae.

Suddenly it rains **gold**... and Zeus visits Danae. How does she feel now? Happy once again.

Nine **months** later, Danae has Zeus's son. She calls him Perseus. 'I can't tell Father about him,' she thinks.

tower a tall building

god an important being who never dies and who decides what happens in the world

gold an expensive yellow metal

month a time of four weeks

READING CHECK

Match the characters from Chapter 1 with the sentences.

| *Danae* | *Zeus* | *Acrisius* | *The priestess* |

a King …*Acrisius*… has no sons.

b ……………… is the king's daughter.

c ……………… goes to Delphi and says, 'I want a son!'

d ……………… says, 'Years from now your grandson kills you.'

e She tells ……………… , 'Don't ask for a son.'

f 'But my daughter can marry and have a boy,' thinks ………………

g Back in Argos, the king puts ……………… in a tower.

h ……………… is the king of the gods.

i He visits ……………… in the tower.

j Nine months later, she has ……………… 's son – Perseus.

GUESS WHAT

What happens in the next chapter? Tick the boxes.

a King Acrisius…

☐ kills Danae and Perseus.

☐ puts Danae and Perseus in the sea.

b Zeus…

☐ takes Danae and Perseus up into the sky.

☐ helps Danae and Perseus across the sea.

c Danae…

☐ marries a good king.

☐ meets a bad king.

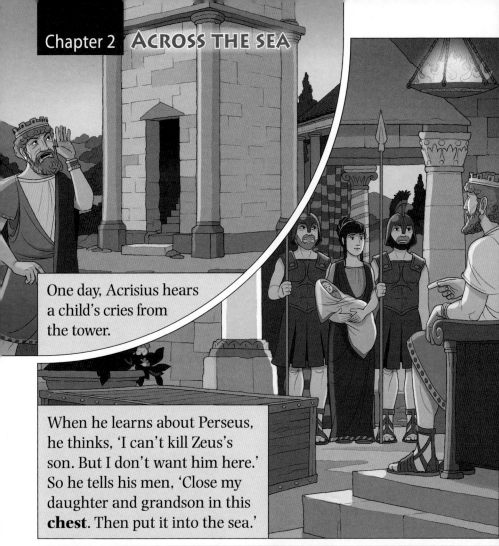

Chapter 2 ACROSS THE SEA

One day, Acrisius hears a child's cries from the tower.

When he learns about Perseus, he thinks, 'I can't kill Zeus's son. But I don't want him here.' So he tells his men, 'Close my daughter and grandson in this **chest**. Then put it into the sea.'

'Help us, Zeus!' Danae cries when they are in the water. Zeus brings the chest **safely** to the **island** of Seriphos.

chest a big box to put things in

safely in a way that nothing bad can happen to somebody

island a country in the sea

A **fisherman** called Dictys opens it. He finds Danae and Perseus.

'My **wife**, Thalia, and I have no children,' Dictys says. 'You two can come and live with us.'

So they stay with the fisherman. When Perseus is older, Dictys teaches the boy many things.

fisherman this man takes fish from the sea

wife a woman living with a man

Dictys's brother Polydectes visits the house when Perseus is a young man. Polydectes is the bad king of Seriphos. He likes Danae. 'Marry me,' he says. 'Mother! Remember Zeus!' Perseus cries. 'I can't marry you,' Danae answers.

Later, Polydectes thinks, 'With Perseus here, I can never marry Danae. What can I do?' Suddenly he smiles. 'I know! I can ask Perseus to a **party**. Then he must bring a **present** – but he has nothing! So I can **send** him away for something. Then I can marry Danae!' he laughs.

party a time when people meet to eat, talk, and drink

present something that you give to someone

send to make someone go somewhere

READING CHECK

Are these sentences true or false? Tick the boxes.

		True	False
a	King Acrisius hears Perseus's laugh.	☐	☑
b	Acrisius can't kill Zeus's son.	☐	☐
c	The king's men put Perseus and Danae in a chest.	☐	☐
d	Zeus takes Perseus and Danae under the sea.	☐	☐
e	Dictys, a teacher on the island of Seriphos, finds them.	☐	☐
f	Dictys's father, Polydectes, is the king of Seriphos.	☐	☐
g	Dictys wants to marry Danae.	☐	☐
h	Danae says, 'I can't marry you.'	☐	☐
i	Polydectes wants to send Perseus away from Danae.	☐	☐

GUESS WHAT

What happens in the next chapter? Tick three sentences.

a King Polydectes asks Perseus to a party. ☐

b Perseus brings a present for the king. ☐

c Perseus kills Polydectes. ☐

d Polydectes kills Perseus. ☐

e The king sends Perseus for a present. ☐

f Polydectes sends Perseus to Acrisius. ☐

g The gods give presents to Perseus. ☐

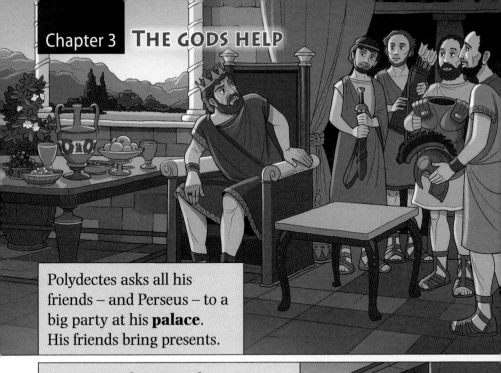

Polydectes asks all his
friends – and Perseus – to a
big party at his **palace**.
His friends bring presents.

But Perseus brings nothing.
'Where's your present for me?'
Polydectes cries angrily.
'What would you like?' Perseus asks.

'Medusa's head,' the king answers.
'Who's Medusa?' Perseus asks.

palace a big house where a king lives

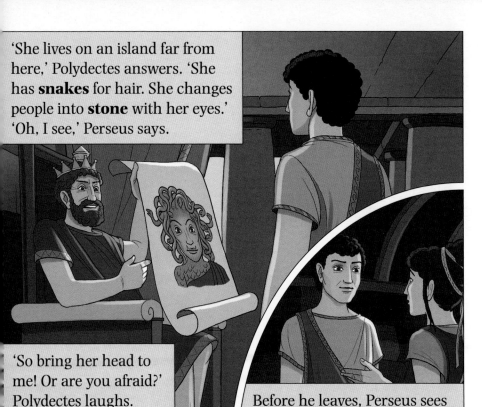

'She lives on an island far from here,' Polydectes answers. 'She has **snakes** for hair. She changes people into **stone** with her eyes.' 'Oh, I see,' Perseus says.

'So bring her head to me! Or are you afraid?' Polydectes laughs. 'No,' Perseus answers. 'I'm going.'

Before he leaves, Perseus sees his mother. Danae says, 'You must ask the gods for help!'

So Perseus goes to the **temple**. The **goddess** Athena and the god Hermes come to him there.

snake a long animal with no legs

stone something grey or white, and hard

temple some people go here to speak to god

goddess a woman god

Athena gives a **shield** to Perseus. 'Look at Medusa in this when you meet,' she says. 'Then she can't change you to stone.'
'But how can I find her?' Perseus asks.

'Go to the island of the **Nymphs** of the **Fountain**. You can **fly** there with these shoes,' Hermes says. 'Come.'

Perseus leaves Seriphos with Hermes.

shield you put this in front of your body to stop people from killing you

nymph a beautiful young woman

fountain water that comes from the ground

fly to move through the sky

READING CHECK

Choose the correct words to complete these sentences.

a King Polydectes asks Perseus to a party in his *palace* / *garden*.

b Perseus brings *nothing* / *a present* for the king.

c Polydectes asks for Medusa's *head* / *hand*.

d Before he leaves Seriphos, Perseus sees his *mother* / *father*.

e Perseus asks the gods for help in the *temple* / *garden*.

f The goddess Athena gives *some shoes* / *a shield* to Perseus.

g The god Hermes gives *some shoes* / *a shield* to Perseus.

h Perseus leaves Seriphos with *Hermes* / *Athena*.

GUESS WHAT

What happens in the next chapter? Tick the boxes.

	Yes	No
a The Fountain Nymphs want to kill Perseus.	☐	☐
b The Nymphs help Perseus.	☐	☐
c They give three presents to him.	☐	☐
d Perseus asks the Nymphs, 'Where's Medusa?'	☐	☐
e They know the answer to the question.	☐	☐
f Perseus must go to a new island and ask there.	☐	☐
g Perseus drinks from the fountain before he leaves.	☐	☐
h He forgets everything and stays with the Nymphs.	☐	☐

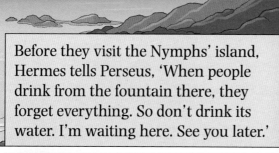

Before they visit the Nymphs' island, Hermes tells Perseus, 'When people drink from the fountain there, they forget everything. So don't drink its water. I'm waiting here. See you later.'

On the island, Perseus tells the Nymphs about his **journey**. They give three presents to him. 'In this hat, you can be **invisible**,' the first Nymph says.
'**Cut off** Medusa's head with this **sickle**,' the second tells him.
'And put it in this bag,' the third smiles.

journey when you go far

invisible when you can't see somebody or something

cut off to take a little thing away from a bigger thing with a knife

sickle people cut long grass with this rounded knife

'Thank you. But where can I find Medusa?' Perseus asks them.
'We don't know,' the first Nymph says.
'Visit the island of the **Grey** Sisters. They know,' the second tells him.
'But before you go, drink from the fountain,' the third smiles.
'No, thank you,' says Perseus. 'I'm not thirsty.'

'Good,' says Hermes when they meet again up in the sky. 'Now let's visit the Grey Sisters.'

grey the colour between white and black

Before they arrive, Hermes tells Perseus, 'The sisters don't like questions, but the three of them see with only one eye. Take it. And after they answer you, they can have it back.'

On the island, Perseus tells the Grey Sisters, 'I'm looking for Medusa. Where's her home?'
'We can't say,' the sister with the eye answers.
'Give the eye to me,' the second sister says. 'I want to see our visitor.'
'Me too,' the third sister cries.

READING CHECK

Correct the mistakes in the sentences.

a Hermes tells Perseus, 'Don't drink the water from the ~~sea!~~' *fountain*

b On the island, Perseus tells the Nymphs about his mother.

c They give money to him.

d 'In this coat, you can be invisible,' the first Nymph says.

e 'Cut off Medusa's hand with this sickle,' the second tells Perseus.

f 'And put it in this chest,' the third smiles.

g Perseus asks, 'Where's Acrisius?' But the Nymphs don't know.

h Perseus goes with Hermes to the island of the Blue Sisters.

i These three sisters have only one mouth.

GUESS WHAT

What happens in the next chapter? Tick two boxes in a, b and c.

a The Grey Sisters…
  1 ☐ lose their eye to Perseus for a time.
  2 ☐ tell Perseus all about Medusa's island.
  3 ☐ go with Perseus to Medusa's island.

b The god Hermes…
  1 ☐ leaves the Grey Sisters' island with Perseus.
  2 ☐ finds Medusa's home for Perseus.
  3 ☐ tells Perseus, 'You must visit Medusa without me!'

c Perseus…
  1 ☐ kills Medusa's sisters.
  2 ☐ sees Medusa in Athena's shield.
  3 ☐ cuts off Medusa's head.

Chapter 5

BAD THINGS
AND GOOD

Suddenly Perseus takes the eye.
'Where's the eye?' the first sister asks.
'I don't know,' the second sister cries.
'He's got it!' the third sister answers.

'You're right,' Perseus
says. 'And you can have
it back. But first answer
my question: Where's
Medusa's island?'
They tell him, and
Perseus gives back the
eye to them.

'Now you must visit Medusa –
alone,' Hermes says. 'Goodbye!'

alone with nobody

When Perseus arrives, he is wearing his hat. He sees Medusa in Athena's shield. But Medusa can't see him. He is invisible.

Quickly he cuts off her head with the sickle. He puts it into his bag.

Then he **takes off** the hat. Suddenly he hears an angry noise. 'Sssssssss!' Medusa's sisters are coming! They can see Medusa's dead body – and Perseus, too!

take off to stop wearing

Perseus flies away fast.

On his journey back home to Seriphos, Perseus sees a young woman. She's in **chains** on some **rocks**. These are near the sea in Ethiopia.

He flies down and asks, 'Who are you? And why are you here?'
'I'm **Princess** Andromeda,' she answers. 'And I'm waiting for a sea **monster**.'
'But why?' Perseus asks.

Andromeda begins, 'I'm more beautiful than the sea god's daughters, Mother says. So Poseidon's angry. And now he's sending Cetus, a hungry monster, for me...'

chains long strings of metal; in these you cannot run away

rock a very big stone

princess the daughter of a king

monster an animal that is very bad to look at

READING CHECK

Put the sentences in order. Number them 1–10.

a ☐ Hermes leaves Perseus.

b ☐ Perseus and the princess talk.

c ☐ Perseus sees Medusa in Athena's shield.

d ☐ Perseus flies away from Medusa's sisters.

e ☐ Perseus cuts off Medusa's head and puts it in his bag.

f ☐ Perseus gives the eye to the Grey Sisters again.

g ☐ Perseus wears his hat and is invisible.

h ☐ Perseus sees Andromeda on some rocks by the sea.

i ☐ Perseus takes the Grey Sisters' eye.

j ☐ The Grey Sisters tell Perseus all about Medusa's island.

GUESS WHAT

What happens in the next chapter? Complete the sentences with the different names.

Acrisius	Andromeda	Danae	Medusa	Perseus	Polydectes

a . . . . kills the sea monster, Cetus.

b Perseus marries . . . .

c Polydectes has a party before he marries . . . .

d Perseus takes . . . . 's head out of his bag at the party.

e . . . . and his men change into stone.

f In the end, Perseus kills his grandfather, ...

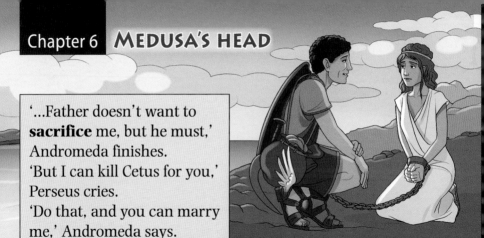

'...Father doesn't want to **sacrifice** me, but he must,' Andromeda finishes.
'But I can kill Cetus for you,' Perseus cries.
'Do that, and you can marry me,' Andromeda says.

Suddenly, Cetus arrives. He's very big.
'Close your eyes, Andromeda!' Perseus cries.
The princess quickly does that.

Perseus takes out Medusa's head from his bag.

Cetus sees it and changes into stone.

sacrifice to kill a person or animal to stop a god being angry

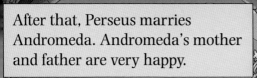

After that, Perseus marries Andromeda. Andromeda's mother and father are very happy.

Then Perseus flies to Seriphos. King Polydectes is having a party. Danae doesn't want to marry him, but she must. 'Your mother's marrying me today. Have you got a present for us?' Polydectes says when Perseus arrives at the party. 'Yes,' Perseus answers. 'Mother, close your eyes!' Danae does this.

Perseus takes out Medusa's head.

Polydectes and his friends see it and change into stone.

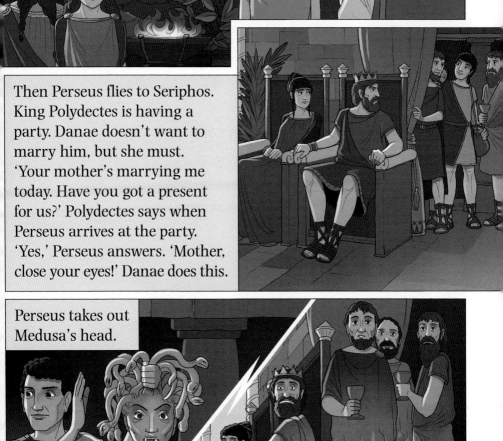

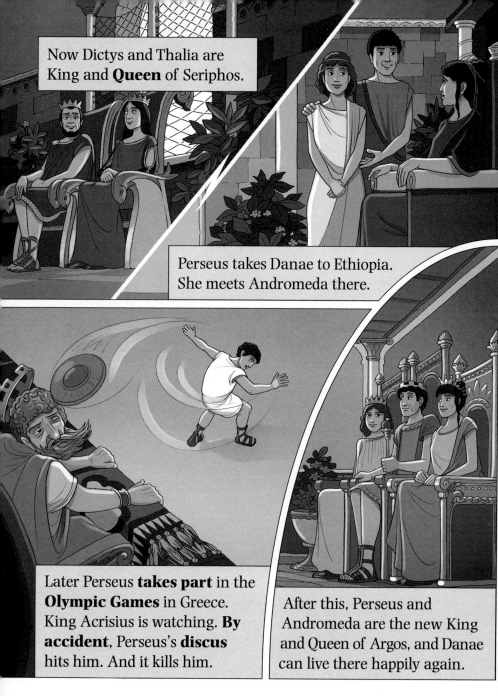

Now Dictys and Thalia are King and **Queen** of Seriphos.

Perseus takes Danae to Ethiopia. She meets Andromeda there.

Later Perseus **takes part** in the **Olympic Games** in Greece. King Acrisius is watching. **By accident**, Perseus's **discus** hits him. And it kills him.

After this, Perseus and Andromeda are the new King and Queen of Argos, and Danae can live there happily again.

queen the wife of a king

take part to do something with other people

Olympic Games important games between different parts of Ancient Greece

by accident not wanting to

discus a round flat thing that you send from your hand through the sky

READING CHECK

1 Choose the correct pictures.

a Who kills Cetus and marries Princess Andromeda?

1 ☐ Acrisius 　　**2** ☑ Perseus 　　**3** ☐ Polydectes

b Who does Polydectes want to marry?

1 ☐ Andromeda 　　**2** ☐ Medusa 　　**3** ☐ Danae

c What kills Polydectes?

1 ☐ sickle 　　**2** ☐ Medusa's eyes 　　**3** ☐ sea monster

d What kills Acrisius?

1 ☐ sickle 　　**2** ☐ Medusa's eyes 　　**3** ☐ discus

2 Choose the correct words to complete the sentences.

a A priestess tells Acrisius 'Don't ask for a *son* / *daughter*!'

b Acrisius's *grandson* / *son* is his killer, she knows.

c *Acrisius* / *Zeus* sends Danae and Perseus away from Argos.

d Later, *Perseus* / *Acrisius* is in the Olympic Games in Greece.

e *Acrisius* / *Perseus* is watching those Olympic Games.

f Perseus kills Acrisius *angrily* / *by accident*.

PROJECTS

Project A Monster-killer heroes

1 Read the text about Perseus and complete the table below.

Perseus comes from Argos in Greece. His father is the god
Zeus and his mother is Princess Danae of Argos.

Perseus cuts off the head of the monster Medusa on her island
home. He changes the sea monster Cetus into stone with the
Medusa's head in the sea near Ethiopia. After that, he marries
Andromeda.

Perseus and Andromeda have seven sons and seven daughters.
Perseus dies quietly in bed when he is an old man!

Who is the hero?	
Where is he from?	
What do we know of his family?	
Which monsters does he kill?	
How and where does he kill them?	
Who does he marry?	
How many children do they have?	
How does Perseus die?	

2 **Read the notes in the table about Beowulf and complete the text about him.**

Who is the hero?	Beowulf
Where is he from?	Geatland, Scandinavia
What do we know of his family?	Ectheow, his father, now dead. Hygelac – Ectheow's brother – King of the Geats
Which monsters does he kill?	The monster Grendel, and Grendel's mother
Where does he kill them?	Grendel – in the Danish King Hrothgar's Great Hall Grendel's mother – in her home under a lake
How does he kill them?	pulls off Grendel's arm with his hands cuts off Grendel's mother's head with a sword
Who does he marry?	Hygd, Hygelac's young wife, after the old king dies
How many children do they have?	no children
How does Beowulf die?	in a fight with a dragon when old

.... comes from .... in .... His father
is .... – now dead – and his uncle is King .... of the
....
.... pulls off the arm of the monster ....
in the Great Hall of the Danish King ....
Then he cuts off the .... of the monster, ..., in
her home under a .... After that, he goes back to Geatland
and marries .... – his uncle Hygelac's young wife – after
.... dies. Beowulf is now King of the .... He and his
wife have .... children. Beowulf dies ....
when he is an old man.

3 **Find out more about a different monster-killer hero. Write his story.**

Gilgamesh and the Giant Humbaba

Glooscap and the Frog Monster

Bellerophon and the Chimera

Siegfried and the Dragon Fafnir

Project B *Riddle poems*

a riddle poem describes something in an unusual way;
the reader or listener must think
carefully to find the answer to the puzzle

1 Read the riddle poem. Which words in each line begin with the same letters? Which thing in the story is it about?

I'm a thin, grey, hungry smile.
I love meeting monsters' necks.
I live in the hero's hand.
I sleep at his side.
I'm afraid of rocks and rain.
Perseus knows me well.
What am I? ....

2 Complete the riddle poem with the words in the box. Which thing in the story is it about?

| bed | flower | priestess | pictures | water |

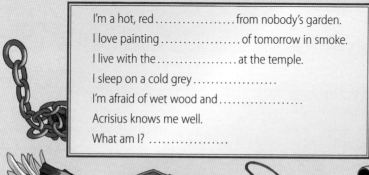

I'm a hot, red .... from nobody's garden.
I love painting .... of tomorrow in smoke.
I live with the .... at the temple.
I sleep on a cold grey ....
I'm afraid of wet wood and ....
Acrisius knows me well.
What am I? ....

3 Choose another thing in the story. Make notes about it in the table.

What do you look like? Use unusual words.	
What do you love?	
Where do you live?	
Where do you sleep?	
What are you afraid of?	
Who in the story knows you well?	
What are you?	

4 Now write a riddle poem about your thing. Use your notes from 3, and the riddle poems in 1 and 2 on page 26, to help you.

> I'm...
> I love...
> I live...
> I sleep..
> I'm afraid of......................................
> .... knows me well.
> Who am I?...

5 Read your riddle poem aloud to the students in your class. They must guess what it's about.

WORD WORK 1

1 These words don't match the pictures. Correct them.

a king....*chest*..... **b** fisherman................. **c** present...................

d island.................. **e** priestess.................. **f** gold..................

g tower.................. **h** chest..................

2 Complete the sentences with words from Chapters 1 and 2.

   a The priestess at Delphi sees things in her $f i r$ e.

   b Danae is in the tower for many [_ o _ _ _ _].

   c The [_ o _] Zeus visits her there,

   d Zeus brings Danae and Perseus [_ a _ e _ _] to Seriphos.

   e The king of Seriphos wants to [_ a _ _ _] Danae.

   f Danae doesn't want to be the [_ i _ e] of Polydectes.

   g Polydectes wants to ask Perseus to a big [_ a _ _ _].

   h He wants to [_ e _ _] Perseus away from Seriphos.

WORD WORK 2

1 Find words from Chapters 3 and 4 to match the pictures.

a temple

b _ _ _ _ _

c _ _ _ _ _ _ _

d _ _ _ _ _ _

e _ _ _ _ _ _

f _ _ _ _ _

g _ _ _ _ _ _ _ _

h _ _ _ _

2 Complete each sentence with a word or phrase from the box.

cuts off	flies	goddess	invisible	journey	Nymphs

a Perseus goes on a long ... journey ... to Medusa's island.

b First, the .... of the Fountain help him, then the Grey Sisters.

c When Perseus puts on his hat, he is ....

d Perseus sees Medusa in the .... Athena's shield,

e He .... the monster's head and puts it in his bag.

f He .... away fast from Medusa's sisters.

WORD WORK 3

1 Find words from Chapters 5 and 6 in the hats to match the pictures.

sencrisp

a p r i n c e s s

hincas

b c _ _ _ _ _ _

enque

c q _ _ _ _ _

sortmen

d m _ _ _ _ _ _

scidus

e d _ _ _ _ _

cork

f r _ _ _

2 Match a word or phrase from the box with the underlined words in each sentence.

> alone.   by accident   sacrifice   takes off   taking part

a Perseus goes and meets Medusa <u>with nobody</u>. ..... alone .....

b When Perseus <u>stops wearing</u> his hat, Medusa's sisters see him. ....

c Poseidon is angry, so Andromeda's father must <u>kill and lose</u> his daughter to the god.
....

d Perseus is <u>doing something</u> in the Olympic Games in Greece....................

e He hits his grandfather <u>but he doesn't want to</u>....................

GRAMMAR CHECK

Yes/No questions and short answers

We use short answers to reply to Yes/No questions.

In a short answer, we re-use the auxiliary verb or the verb be from the question.

Does Acrisius want a son?   *Yes, he does.*

Is he happy after he visits Delphi?   *No, he isn't. (is not)*

1 **Write answers for the questions about Danae. Use the short answers in the box.**

> No, she can't.   Yes, it does.   No, she hasn't.   No, she isn't.   Yes, she can.
> Yes, she does.   Yes, she has.   ~~Yes, she is.~~   Yes, she is.

a Is she Acrisius's only daughter? ...Yes, she is.......

b Has she got any brothers? ....

c Is she from Seriphos? ....

d Does she live in a tower for a time? ....

e Can she meet young men there? ....

f Does it rain gold when Zeus first visits her?

....

g Is she happy when she has Perseus? ....

h Has she got friends on Seriphos? ....

i Can she go back to Argos in the end?

....

2 **Now write short answers to these questions about Perseus.**

a Is he from Argos? ....

b Is he the god Poseidon's son? ....

c Can he look into Medusa's eyes? ....

d Can he fly through the sky? ....

e Has he got a sickle, a hat, and a bag?

....

f Has he got snakes for hair? ....

g Does he marry Andromeda? ....

h Does he change his grandfather into stone?

....

GRAMMAR CHECK

Questions with question words, or 'information questions'

We use question words – like who, what, why, where, when, how, how far, how many – in information questions. We answer these questions by giving information.

Why does Acrisius send Danae and Perseus away? Because he's afraid of his grandson.

What's the name of Dictys's wife? Thalia.

How many gods does Perseus meet on Seriphos? Two.

3 Complete the information questions with the question words in the box.

How	How far	How many	What	When	Where	Which	~~Who~~	Who	Why

a Q: ......Who...... is Dictys?

A: A fisherman on the island of Seriphos.

b Q: .... do Danae and Perseus arrive on Seriphos?

A: By sea, in a big chest.

c Q: .... is Polydectes?

A: The bad King of Seriphos.

d Q: .... does Polydectes first meet Danae?

A: When he comes to visit his brother, Dictys.

e Q: .... does Perseus need to leave Seriphos?

A: Because King Polydectes asks him for Medusa's head.

f Q: .... does Danae say when she hears of this?

A: 'You must ask the gods for help, Perseus!'

g Q: .... does Perseus meet Hermes and Athena?

A: In the temple on Seriphos.

h Q: .... presents do the gods give to Perseus?

A: Two – a shield and some shoes.

i Q: .... present is from Athena?

A: The shield.

j Q: .... is Medusa's island from Seriphos?

A: Very far.

GRAMMAR CHECK

Imperatives

We make the imperative using the infinitive without *to*. We put *don't* before the verb to make the negative imperative.

Ask the Nymphs of the Fountain for their help.

Don't look into Medusa's eyes.

Don't wait! Kill her quickly!

4 **Complete the sentences with the imperative form of the verbs in the box.**

> be   have   ~~not drink~~   not forget   take   tell   visit

a '...Don't drink... the water!' Hermes tells Perseus.

b '........................the Nymphs about your journey!' Hermes says to him.

c '........................these nice presents with you!' the Nymphs tell Perseus.

d '........................the island of the Grey Sisters!' the Nymphs say to him.

e '........................a drink from the fountain!' they tell him before he goes.

f '........................careful!........................about the water,' Hermes says to Perseus.

5 **What do the Grey Sisters tell Perseus? Complete the sentences.**

> arrive   cut off   ~~fly~~   stop   leave   not make   not stay   put   watch   wear

a) ....Fly....... north from here for a day.

b) .... when you see an island of tall, grey rocks. That's Medusa's home.

c) .... our hat when you fly down to it. d) .... invisibly on the island.

e) .... Medusa in Athena's shield.

f) .... any noise. g) ....the monster's head with your sickle.

h) .... her head in your bag.

i) .... long on the island.

j) .... quickly before Medusa's sisters find you.

DOMINOES Your Choice

Read *Dominoes* for pleasure, or to develop language skills. It's your choice.

Each *Domino* reader includes:
- a good story to enjoy
- integrated activities to develop reading skills and increase vocabulary
- task-based projects – perfect for CEFR portfolios
- contextualized grammar activities

Each *Domino* pack contains a reader, and an excitingly dramatized audio recording of the story

If you liked this *Domino*, read these:

The Selfish Giant
Oscar Wilde

'It's my garden,' says the Giant. 'People must understand! Nobody can play here – only me!'

So the children leave, and the Selfish Giant puts a wall around his garden. After that, it's always winter there.

Later, the Giant feels sorry for a young boy in the snow. He knocks down the garden wall – and the children, and the spring, come back. But where is the young boy now? And how can the Giant find him again?

Ali Baba and the Forty Thieves
Retold by Janet Hardy-Gould

After Ali Baba finds a thieves' treasure cave, he is suddenly rich. Then his brother Kasim visits the cave, and things go wrong. The forty thieves find Kasim there, kill him, and cut his body into four pieces. What can Ali Baba do? He wants to bury his brother quietly. But how can he? Morgiana, his servant-girl, has the answer. But what can she do when the thieves find Ali Baba and want to kill him, too?

	CEFR	Cambridge Exams	IELTS	TOEFL iBT	TOEIC
Level 3	B1	PET	4.0	57-86	550
Level 2	A2–B1	KET-PET	3.0-4.0	–	390
Level 1	A1–A2	YLE Flyers/KET	3.0	–	225
Starter & Quick Starter	A1	YLE Movers	1.0–2.0	–	–

You can find details and a full list of books and teachers' resources on our website:
www.oup.com/elt/gradedreaders